the Little Book of
MINDSET
MATTERS

Joseph S. Maniscalco

the Little Book of
MINDSET
MATTERS

Joseph S. Maniscalco

CHAMPS

Printed and Electronic Versions
ISBN Paperback 978-1-956353-73-0
ISBN Hardback 978-1-956353-74-7
ISBN eBook 978-1-956353-75-4
(Joseph S. Maniscalco / Motivation Champs)

The book was printed in the United States of America.

To order additional copies or bulk order contact the publisher,
Motivation Champs Publishing.
www.motivationchamps.com

DELIVERABLES

INTRODUCTION

Who among us hasn't dreamed? Hasn't savored the future? Hasn't wanted something so badly it hurt? And when you can almost touch it, almost feel it, it was gone. The exaltation of the dream, the anguish of the loss. We have all felt it—the best and worst of life.

It was August 1991, and I had recently signed a one-page contract to try out for the Los Angeles Dodgers the following spring. My dream was in front of me. My opportunity the following spring of what could be. Having been told to take the summer off and not pitch, my listening skills did not work. Instead, I continued to compete in a collegiate summer league. I had just come off a great season as a junior in college and desired the continued competition. Fast forward to a beautiful night at Mitchell Park under the lights, pitching with the backdrop of the summer sun coming down. The air was crisp but warm, and the environment was a baseball player's dream. Two teams competing in the last weekend before summer ball ends and then heading back to college. In an instant, the entire path of my future changed. In an instant, the wind-up and the pitch changed the course of everything that would happen the following year. The same warm-up. The same wind-up. The same mechanics. All these done thousands of times before, led to a grimace on a particular pitch. Not having experienced anything like it, I threw another pitch and then felt a weakened, dead arm. Coming out of the game was nothing short of internal devastation. My mind raced with thoughts. Scrambled eggs in my head, mixed with scrambled feelings and emotions of what happened, what will happen, and what my future will be. A future dedicated to a sport I loved internally more than anything in the world. To a sport that resonated with me on a different level than most. The love and passion to play each and every day were present in the way I approached the game. Now, in an instant, it may be over.

For as long as my memory goes back, I have had a deep interest in the universe, philosophy, and the mind. As a student, I would sometimes over analyze simple reasoning concepts because my mind was wandering about nature, the philosophies of God, and the universe. Along the way, this habit unknowingly became my strength. As an average student in a rigorous all-boys high school, I worked really hard to get good grades; suffice to say, high school subjects did not come naturally to me. Frustration sometimes led to temporary disappointment, but I continued to focus my mind on being just a "little bit better."

In my high school, they would post this big board in the hallway entrance with the names of the students who had made the honor roll for the prior semester. That was the first thing visitors saw when they walked into the school. The vision of my name one day being inscribed for the semester on that board guided me through the long nights of studying. At the time, I was a student athlete; I loved sports and clubs and had a vivid comedic imagination. This made the natural brainiac tendencies of most, which I did not possess, really show up during exams. I made that board a couple of times in four years. It felt great for the semester, only to feel the disappointment the next semester when I missed the mark by .01. The point is that we all go through these difficult failures in pursuit of success, but it is in that process that I became the person I am today. We are shaped by those failures and experiences, and the resilience created by encountering these things. Sometimes, I joke that I finally feel smart – it only took 50 years.

For those of you who have not experienced those failures and are elite scholars, I stand up and applaud you and wish you a lifetime of peace of mind. For the rest of us commoners, as Marcus Aurelius said, "Life is a warfare, and a stranger's sojourn, and after fame is oblivion." Essentially, we were all made of dust and will return there one day.

While I am formally educated and have an undergraduate degree from Fordham University, B.A. (Journalism and Philosophy), and a law degree from Hofstra University, J.D., the most practical guided experience was learned in an all-boys catholic high school called Chaminade, followed up through my life experiences; falling, getting up, showing up, again, learning, and then failing again, but then showing up again with a stronger mindset. Through patience, resilience, and my Faith in God, I was able to get through the most difficult times. You can do the same. Perhaps the best education one can receive is called the School of Hard Knocks.

I feel a strong pull to use my knowledge and resources in this space. I feel a presence from God and a responsibility to serve, help, guide, and teach as much as possible, and change a perspective, mindset, thought pattern, or future. This responsibility and gravitational pull have been with me for some time. Now is the time. This is the Way.

As you read this little book, embrace the unknown, visualize your dreams and future, and understand that a strong mindset is a way of life – a choice – a decision – a commitment. It is a perspective that will launch positivity and creativity to heights you have never imagined. And when your mind and body come together, your performance will transcend to places and outcomes that bring joy, but more importantly, fulfillment. If you embrace this new understanding, you will be unrecognizable to the outside world, but in a much more productive and peaceful way.

As you read, I encourage you to reflect, smile, take notes, underline things that appeal to you, and use the concepts and teachings in your daily life. Practice on the world. See how it responds. Be yourself and the person you were meant to be, and have a blast along the way. Remember, nothing is permanent; live in the present, make mistakes, get up, dust yourself off, learn from them, journal, meditate, and pray because, in the end, it all works out the way it is supposed to, according to God's plan.

What do I ask of you, the reader? If you enjoy this, have learned from it, or it has captured your heart, share it and pay it forward. We all have a responsibility to learn and then share. Please pay it forward to the youth, the innocent and naïve ones who don't yet understand how their thoughts and desires can create a scrambled mind. And then, ask them to do the same, and so on and so on.

Together, we can create a better mindset for all because, in the end, Mindset Matters.

Change Your Mindset.

Change Your Life.

When You Change Your Mindset, Everything Changes.

Let the Journey Begin.

CREATE YOUR FOUNDATION

At the core of everything, there is a foundation. Find your foundation. What is your strength? You can accomplish this by finding your core values and then living those core values. When the going gets tough, look to the core values as they are the foundation. If the foundation cracks and you deviate from your values, gaps emerge, and outside stimuli seep in, forcing a separation of the foundation. Once that occurs, the gaps become wider, and every opinion flows in like an open fire hydrant, and you become unable to decipher anything. This leads the mind to paralysis of analysis and a storm of inconsistency, confusion, and continued consternation.

Think of a home. Think of a skyscraper. Think of the pyramids. These structures all start with a Foundation. In a world where humans are humans and their emotions, feelings, trust, and loyalty can switch very quickly, having a Foundation in God provides me with unconditional comfort. For me, Jesus will always be there no matter what – timeless, caring, loving, supportive, adaptive, forgiving, and peaceful. I have yet to find all those qualities and characteristics wrapped in one anywhere else.

If you were to ask me what was the single thing that got me through, it was simply God, my Faith and belief, and a whole lot of prayer. For me, that is where my Foundation starts and ends. For you, it can be any place you desire, but find it.

DEVELOP YOUR ROOTS AND NOTHING CAN TOPPLE YOU

Have you ever heard of the lotus flower? It is a symbol of purity, enlightenment, and rebirth. Its characteristics are a great analogy for the human condition; even when its roots are in the dirtiest waters, the lotus produces the most beautiful flower. It starts deep beneath the water and in the darkness and dirt, only to rise up from those strong roots. That lotus flower sprouts up from the mud and through the water to emerge above the water, looking into the sun. It starts, however, with the roots. It starts with the grasp of those roots deep into the ground.

Did you know that Redwood trees grow over 300 feet in the air with a width span of 22 feet at their base, and are considered the largest and tallest trees in the world? Interestingly, the roots go down 10-13 feet deep before spreading outward 60-80 feet. They tangle the roots into grooves, which provides additional strength. Due to the strength of their root system and environment, they are said to have been here for thousands of years. The root system is the reason for the strength of the Redwood trees. The root system is the foundation of the Redwood tree, and the tangling of those roots creates the strength that allows it to reach high into the sky.

Developing a strong foundation and root system is at the core of creating a strong and impenetrable mindset. In the end, Mindset Matters.

CHANGE YOUR VOCABULARY

In the beginning, there was the Word, and the Word was God. The spoken word has the power to build up and rip down in the same instant. The word has the power to be uplifting to you and beat you down with anxiety and worry. The words spoken to yourself and to others should be guarded. It is the most important superpower you have. And it has been provided to each and every human in one form or another.

The words we speak are profound and deep and can penetrate a person's heart, or lift them to the highest place. Words have an impact. Words have meaning. They can be used as a sword or a shield. They can be more emotionally powerful to someone using them the right way than any other source. Studying words and their impact, I realized there was a direct connection between words and the brain. The brain hears the words, deciphers them with truth, and then absorbs them into the mind. In doing this, it can have a profound impact on the way the person responds.

High-performance individuals have a different vocabulary. They do not use words like "I can't," "This sucks," "She's yelling at me," or "I stink." Instead, they reframe that vocabulary into something productive, forward-thinking, and worthwhile. If you allow negative words to permeate your mind, you will be damaging the mind, leading to a poor result.

High-performance people are not cynical. They respect all but fear none. Instead of the "I can't" vocabulary, they use words like "I can't wait to figure this out," "I love this challenge," and "This will take time to succeed." High-performance individuals are success-conscious, positive people who look to gratitude and reframe their vocabulary. They understand the meaning and importance of the spoken Word.

You will not find many negative, successful people, but you will find an abundance of positive, successful people.

Change Your Vocabulary!

CHANGE WHAT YOU SEE

What you see is all about perspective. Your eyes are the window to your world. Perspective is all about how you feel internally, resulting from your environment, your circle of strength, and the people who support you. With perspective, aim to see opportunity. Aim to see through a prism of gratitude, a positive attitude, and a forward-thinking mindset. In doing so, you will see what others don't. And when that happens, you will forge the MindBody (when the heart, mind and body are aligned) connection to be the best version of yourself in anything you do.

There is a story about two shoe salesmen who were sent to an undeveloped country and asked to report back on whether there were any opportunities. The first one went, looked around, and saw that no one wore shoes. He reported back to the company—no one wears shoes here, and there are no opportunities. The second one reported back—no one wears shoes here. Glorious opportunity!

We have a tendency to make assumptions and see things negatively. When this happens, stop, pause, and change what you see. As you change your view, your perspective changes. Remember, your perspective will always become your reality.

Change What You See!

CHANGE WHAT YOU HEAR

God created us all with two ears and one mouth. There is a reason; seek to listen twice as much as you speak. By changing what you hear, you reframe the words of someone else. If you hear negative, you will react negatively. If you listen carefully and reframe it, your MindBody connection will respond differently. This requires conscious awareness of thought. In that conscious awareness, you have all the power.

Between stimulus and response lies the freedom to decide what you hear and how you will respond. That space in between is in your control and represents your complete freedom. As you hear something, make sure you are not clouding or adding words, tone, and effect to satisfy your negative conclusion. Listen carefully, absorb, and reframe what you hear to translate into the mind something forward-thinking. This will change your mindset of what you hear, which will change everything because Mindset Matters.

Change What You Hear!

BE THE BEST VERSION
OF YOURSELF
AND NOTHING MORE

One of the most important principles I learned at Chaminade was to seek to be the best version of yourself. I will never forget the words of Brother Genovese [paraphrased] – "It doesn't matter what you become. It matters who you become. Do not place a label on what you become, but rather, be the best version of yourself and always improve upon who you become. Whether you are a street sweeper or the CEO of a major company, be the best at that job – that is your vision and goal, gentlemen."

If you merely seek to be the best version of yourself and show up with that best version, you will have the ability to look yourself in the mirror and feel peace. We all seek peace of mind in the duty of our actions. Those who cannot find that peace of mind continue along the journey, confused and paralyzed. To find that peace of mind, simply look to be the best version of yourself each day in all that you do. It really is that simple.

YOU GET TO DO LIFE
SO LOVE WHAT YOU DO

Life is about the simple pleasures of the experiences we encounter. The sun will rise each day as sure as you will breathe oxygen to fuel your cells. As we go through the day, we often paralyze our minds with thoughts of why this is happening to us. Things don't actually happen to you. Things happen for you. You don't have to do anything in life; it's all a choice based on a calculation of different things. You do, however, get to experience life. You get to experience school. You get to experience sports, friends, a social life, and everything in between. Once you reframe that mindset and consistently use these words, they emit a feeling of gratitude, and we know that gratitude is at the top of the Mindset Matters list of deliverables.

You cannot be successful in anything unless you love what you do. I built a girls' softball program on the following: Play for the Love of the Game and look to Exceed Expectations. That was the principle we played by; it was not winning every tournament and game. Simply love what you do and look to exceed expectations. We loved practice. We loved to play. We loved to compete. Sometimes we succeeded, and sometimes we failed. But we kept going and continued to love the game. In doing that, the standards we created were high, as we wanted to exceed the expectations, and we loved what we did, which helped in the tough times. Because it's the tough times that define us— how we respond to those— how we react— how we behave when the tough times rear their ugly head.

Each business I have built was done and cultivated on a foundation of passion and love for that business. But for that, each would not have exceeded my expectations. There is no doubt in my mind that they would not have been successful. Each time I brought love, energy, effort, a positive attitude, and passion to the business, it succeeded. There were times when a business didn't sustain the long haul. Reflecting back, it was a direct result of a loss of love, passion, positive attitude, gratitude, and belief. When those were lost, the entire environment changed, and the business faltered.

It's like the age-old adage, "If you love what you do, you will never work a day in your life."

Follow the path of love, as God is love. God is the supply.

NO ONE REMEMBERS EASY

Life is a daily grind. We rise each day and have an opportunity to seek the best of life and the best of ourselves. This is the greatest opportunity we are afforded. When we go through this thing called life, we get to see what we can do and we get to see where we can take ourselves. We don't have to, but rather, we get to.

If you look at any great and wonderful thing received in life or achieved, the best of it was always through hard work and a grind. No one remembers easy. Think of every achievement; the ones you tell stories about were those you fought really hard for, because no one remembers easy.

While we may seek easy, the path of suffering and hard work is always the way. Learn this early in life, and you will tell stories of the greatness that is in you while you look inward and find the way to bring it to life.

The paradox of suffering to gain strength is difficult to embrace. It is quite the opposite of our natural tendencies. Experiencing discomfort trains the mind to recognize what may seemingly be the unknown and prevent the mind from panicking. In the voluntary act of engaging in discomfort, we train the mind, body and spirit and strengthen an attitude of perseverance and determination. And when we survive these uncomfortable experiences, the result becomes glorious, liberating and all worthwhile. Because, in the end, no one remembers easy.

YOU ARE THE BOSS OF THE BANK MAKE GOOD DEPOSITS

Visualize a Bank. Visualize going to the bank and depositing your money each day. The bank holds your money for you, and when you want it, you go to the bank, and it provides you with the money, with a little interest as well for holding it.

Think of your mind in the same way. You get to make deposits each day. You can deposit positive ideas, images, and thoughts into your memory bank, as well as negative ones. Now, think, you are the boss of the bank, and all the employees listen to you and are very loyal. When you need some advice or help making a decision, you ask the employees to withdraw deposits you previously made, and they will give you back exactly what you deposited.

When withdrawals are made from the bank based on the deposits you previously made, the bank employees return to you exactly what you previously provided in deposits. There is no change in the way you made the deposits because the employees listen and provide the information right back to you.

This brings us to the importance of our daily deposits. Feed your bank (mind) with a daily dose of good deposits, and the bank (mind) will give you the same withdrawals.

As Marcus Aurelius once said, "The happiness of your life depends upon the quality of your thoughts."

THE MIND DOES NOT
DISCRIMINATE

Thoughts, images, and ideas are constantly presented through our eyes and ears. The mind takes that information in and does not compartmentalize it to determine which part is negative and which is positive, which part should be used, and which part should be discarded. Instead, the mind takes the information in and causes a vibration of feelings based upon that information. That information can literally transform our reality. This is why we must feed the mind a steady diet of positive information. By doing so, we train and prevent the mind from accumulating negative "I can't," "I'm afraid," "I am scared," and "This is tough" information.

Look at a dictionary definition of discrimination, and this is what you will find: "recognition and understanding of the difference between one thing and another," and "discrimination between right and wrong." The mind does not recognize and understand the difference between one thing and another, and send back a signal that this is a negative thought, and you should not use it. Instead, the mind focuses on what you focus on. It then translates those signals to the body in performance.

The mind does not discriminate by recognizing and understanding the difference between a good thought and a bad one. The mind absorbs the information you feed it and cannot simply dissect it and say this is right and wrong – don't worry about this negative stuff because I will just keep it in the corner for you. The mind takes the information in, and it becomes part of your thoughts and behaviors. It is up to us to provide good content, information, and data for our minds so that our responses move us forward.

We do not understand the method by which our brains use each and every circumstance and transmit desire into physical action, but we know that by feeding your mind the right types of images and thoughts, you can train it. With social media and the internet, our minds are flooded with a vast amount of information. Be careful with what we feed our minds. We know the mind ingests what we feed it and absorbs the information, which has a cause and effect on the physical body. Why? I believe the mind and body work together, and the body merely translates the mind's vocabulary. By having the vocabulary driven by words of desire and belief, the body moves in that same direction and in that vibration.

Feeding the mind with a consistent dose of rich nutrition will translate into a more productive MindBody connection because, in the end, Mindset Matters.

YOU ARE THE MASTER OF YOUR FATE AND THE CAPTAIN OF YOUR SOUL

As Napoleon Hill proclaims in Think and Grow Rich when poet William Ernest Henley wrote the prophetic lines in his poem Invictus, "I am the Master of my Fate, I am the Captain of my Soul," he was speaking way before the time of the population explosion and understood the power of the mind. He understood that we "have the ability" or can control what is fed to our brains by the activities we undertake and the feelings we exemplify. The mind and its amazing power make no attempt to discriminate between destructive and constructive thoughts. Just as quickly as it influences us to act upon thoughts of success, it can urge us to translate thoughts of loss and defeat into physical reality. As Napoleon Hill describes, "that by means which no one fully understands, these dominating thoughts, like magnetics, attract to us the forces, the people, the circumstances of life which harmonize with the nature of our dominating thoughts. Our brains become "magnetized" with the dominating thoughts we hold in our minds."

Before we can accumulate success in great abundance, we must magnetize our minds with an intense desire for success. We must become success-conscious until the desire for success drives us to create definite plans for acquiring it, and we consciously work on feeding that desire with the proper nutrition and ingredients. You can't grow a strong oak tree with a broken seed; the same way you cannot develop a strong mind by instilling fear, doubt, or insecurity.

LEARN TO TALK TO YOURSELF

There is a great story about Dr. James Gills, the only person on the planet to complete six double Ironman Triathlons.

When asked how he did it, he said, "I learned to talk myself instead of listen to myself. If I listen to myself, I will hear all the fear, doubt, and excuses of why I cannot finish this. It will feed me all the reasons why this cannot be done. If I talk to myself, I can feed myself with the words of encouragement I need to keep on moving forward. Talking to myself allows me to visualize a future event or goal."

The thoughts we think and the words we say become our reality and the life that we create. They create our perspective, which becomes our reality. What we say, think, and believe matters. Our Mindset Matters. We need to breathe life into the words we speak to ourselves. That creates a vibration of moving forward, allowing the body to keep going.

If we hear whining, complaining and other words that prevent growth, the listening can overwhelm. When you talk to yourself and visualize a great outcome, you resonate the MindBody connection to a more productive place.

Talk to yourself with words of encouragement, growth, abundance and gratitude because your mind is listening.

LOOK, LISTEN AND LEARN

I call this the three Ls approach. The good Lord gave you two ears and one mouth. In the perfect creation of us human beings, God must have thought that His humans should do a great deal of listening. Listen twice as much as you speak. Adapt, understand, and absorb information. Pick people you respect, understand, and are grateful for, and gravitate to those people so you can develop a foundation of understanding them.

Many of us speak first, speak often, and don't really understand what we say. We forget the point of the argument and sometimes forget the entire point altogether. This is due to a culture that tells you to be heard. I am a proponent of being heard, but you first need to listen and understand to be understood. If your mouth is rambling with no point or destination, how can you honestly be understood?

Look, Listen and Learn.

TAKE THE FIRST STEP

Simple yet profound. "A journey of a thousand miles starts with a single step." As said by philosopher Lao Tzu 2,000 years ago, it provides great insight into our thought process. Our human minds often look way past the event far into the future, and then we become paralyzed. We think of all the reasons it cannot go as planned. In doing so, we do nothing. Paralysis of the future event causes inaction due to the uncertainty of the future result.

Take a single step towards life. Don't look way down the line because it will permeate your mind, create doubt, and seem overwhelming. You don't want to feel overwhelmed; you want to feel empowered, part of the experience, and light on your feet. What is the sense of doing it if you're not going to enjoy the process along the way?

Take the first step. When that is done, think the same way and take another step. If you journey towards and complete a thousand-mile walk, remember that it all started with a single step.

IT IS A JOURNEY, NOT A SPRINT

Have you ever heard the phrase, stop and smell the roses? Have you ever thought about it? Our culture and society are such that people lack patience. This is clearly a product of social media, which I call the sword and the shield of life. It has created a culture of immediate reaction. People need to post and have a burning desire to tell the world and everyone who will listen that they are happy and successful. Indeed, and interestingly, no one ever posts about their failures. Have you ever read a post about messing up or doing poorly? I doubt it.

Life is a journey not a sprint. Embrace the journey. Experience the journey. Cultivate the journey. Breathe life into the journey. Be patient in the journey and try to enjoy the process along the way. Don't expect results every second, every day, and, for athletes, every game. Don't define your life by success, but rather by becoming better each day. The accumulation of small daily victories creates the MindBody connection.

Win, lose, cry, cheer, smile, embarrass yourself, enjoy the moment, learn, develop, adapt, grow, remember, talk about it, and do it again.

Trust, faith, and patience are the ultimate sacrifices in reaching the goal. Enjoy the journey and experience inner peace.

WRITE YOUR OWN SCRIPT

Sometimes, we forget that life is an abundance of limitless opportunities. We can live the life we have imagined by moving in the direction of our dreams. You have a blank canvas each day. There are very few guarantees in life, but one is that the sun will rise tomorrow. With a new day each day, you have a new opportunity to do something great every single day. What a feeling! I am always grateful for that.

How will your story read? How will it end? What will it be like? Will it be glorious? Will it be great? If you dream it, then see it, write it down, and fuel it with a strong Belief and Desire, it has the highest tendency of becoming a reality. This I tell you with a great deal of confidence.

People who have no vision are lost in a forest of trees without the ability to see the end. Great moments are created from great opportunities. However, great opportunities are first created by great thought, vision, writing, and then action.

If you bet on yourself and wrote your own script, you have no excuses or anything to blame. And when you write your script, you naturally create inner peace because you live the life you choose and desire.

Use your positve mindset to write your script.

DON'T WHINE.
DON'T COMPLAIN.
DON'T MAKE EXCUSES.

— Jimmy Valvano

An inspirational speech was given by Jimmy Valvano at the Espy Awards shortly before he lost his bout with cancer. The takeaway was one of the most profound things I've ever heard.

He told his players:

> Don't Whine.
>
> Don't Complain.
>
> Don't Make Excuses.
>
> Just Play the Game.

Simple, yet deeply impactful.

Reflection on each word provides great insight and opportunity into how to carry yourself each day. Not whining enables you to take responsibility for everything that occurs to you. Those who regularly whine usually stunt their personal growth as they fail to take responsibility. By not complaining, you provide a mind that thinks in the present and moves forward as opposed to reflecting on the past. And finally, excuses are the thief of accountability. Arnold Schwarzenegger points out that, "You can have results or excuses, but not both."

Take these timeless principles and watch how well the future of your life unfolds.

BEWARE OF PARALYSIS
OF ANALYSIS

Many people go through life analyzing every situation. Athletes do this all the time, and they complain. (I think too much. I can't get out of my head. Why do I think so much?) People with left-brain dominance are very analytical. The problem is that their thinking leads to more thinking. In doing this, they rarely take action. Instead, they simply wait for something to happen, and then they actually think some more.

You can read countless books on training, performance, and try to learn all the secrets of success. However, nothing will guide, push, develop, or enable you to learn until you do something and take action. I can tell you what to do. I can teach you what to do. I can give you stories and show you success, but you will not be ready until you embrace the belief and free your mind of analysis.

John F. Kennedy once said, "This country has made more mistakes on indecision than the wrong decision." Over analyzing leads to paralysis. Paralysis is a state of non-movement. Our lives must always move, especially for athletes. Seek to learn, always. There is no way you can be the person you envision yourself to be unless you act, do, fail, make mistakes, and then get up and learn and do it again.

When we take action and make a decision, we consciously move the mind in the direction of that decision. When that decision does not pan out the way we anticipate, it triggers the mind to think, "Yikes, no good." We then either accept that decision and try to adjust or make an excuse. The key, however, is that in the decision-making, there is learning. And in learning, there is growth and development.

As Yoda said, "Do or do not. There is no try."

WE EXPERIENCE
WHAT WE FOCUS ON

In life, we usually experience what we focus on. You cannot control the external circumstances, events, and opinions of others or how they react or respond to things. Whatever you focus on, you are going to feel, even if it is not true. We often make the mistake of living in the untruthful nature of external forces. Instead, train your mind and be better at focusing on the positive aspects of life and the present situation.

You can control what you do with your body and mind. After focus comes belief. If you believe something to be true, it is usually true, even if the evidence says otherwise, until you challenge the assessment of your belief. If you don't challenge the assessment of the belief, evidence will suddenly show up consistent with your focus and your belief, and satisfy the mind that what you focused on and believed was true. This is a double-edged sword, but you can use it against the world of cynical conclusions and benefit from the thinking.

Focus on positivity, growth, learning, gratitude, abundance, love, and faith, and believe in that focus. All of a sudden, your life will become a series of positive, growth-inspiring, experiences filled with Love, Faith, and Abundance.

Remember, we don't experience life. We experience the life we focus on and believe.

USE POSITIVE SELF-TALK

Language is important, universal, and timeless. We each speak in our native tongue, and while one may not understand the language of another, the language of each of us is crucial to how we communicate with the world and how the world receives information and responds to us.

Be careful of the language you use toward yourself. Words have power; they can lift up or break down. They have the power to encourage or discourage. They have the power to move forward or remain stagnant. Whether speaking out loud or silently to ourselves, how we form thoughts impacts our emotions and behavior. Language shapes how we see the world and ourselves in it, how we move through it, and how we react to it. Then, the recipient of the language we use is shaped, and their response and behavior to our language occurs.

Bruce Lee once said, "Don't speak negatively about yourself, even as a joke. Your body doesn't know the difference. Words are energy, and they cast spells; that's why it's called spelling." Change the way you speak about yourself, and you can change your life.

If we are not careful, bad habits can seep into our vernacular. Words and phrases used negatively on ourselves can become debilitating. That energy flow you just delivered will surround you and create your behavior. So, take care with the words you speak to yourself. As James Gills, the Ironman Athlete I mentioned earlier, spoke positive words to himself, he completed what seemed to be an impossibility.

Language exerts hidden power, and we are armed with power, so be careful how you use the power of your words on yourself. They can change your life for the better or hurt it.

What you are not changing, you are choosing.

SERVICE TO OTHERS
IS THE GOLDEN TICKET

In a new age world where social media dominates the space between our ears, it's important to keep in perspective and in balance with who you are as a person. How we treat others says more about who we are than any one thing we can do. Service to others is the golden ticket.

We are defined by what we do for others. What have you done for someone else lately? A person's true worth is not about their status in the world or the things they have accumulated but how they treat others. Watch how people treat others, and you will find the special ones, the ones who you want to emulate.

It's about the positive impact you leave on the world and those around you. Respect and humility never go out of style. The change you want to see in the world must start with you. Be reminded that every person you meet has value, no matter what they look like or what they do for a living. Value is the foundation of their inner soul. And who are we to take away someone's value or reach into their soul?

DON'T LET THE CHAOS AROUND YOU AFFECT YOUR INNER PEACE

You can only control yourself. The outside world and external events of society will always be there. As each day you take a breath and are guaranteed that the sun will rise, there will always be external forces of nature and events that will look to disrupt your mind. Don't allow the chaos around you to affect your inner peace. It is important to keep who you are as a person in perspective and balance. This is done by controlling the things you can control.

Inner peace is within your control. Control what you can control and nothing else. You can control you. You can control your attitude, energy and the way you show up each day. You can control your response to events. You can control how you treat others, how you speak to others, and how you serve others. You cannot control how others treat you, their opinions, or their reactions. You cannot control their responses to events. Meditation, walking, exercising, reading a book, or being reminded of the beauty of nature all help with your inner peace and remind you to control what you can control.

"Everyone thinks of changing the world, but no one thinks of changing themselves." Leo Tolstoy.

Look inward, and don't allow the chaos to pay rent in your mind. Evict the chaos!

HEAT AND PRESSURE
ARE A NECESSITY
IN DIFFICULT TIMES

Bad times are made for good people. That means when times get tough, good things actually start to happen and show up in our lives. The need for immediate gratification should take a pause to allow the tough times to work through the mind so that the good starts to show up. As an example, what takes the wrinkle out of your shirt or pants? Heat and pressure of the iron. What turns a dark piece of coal into a polished, beautiful diamond? Heat and pressure. When the times get tough, through your Faith, patience, and gratitude, you will find that the wrinkles get smoothed out and the diamonds start to take shape; and then, suddenly, the brilliant light of Jesus shines as we walk with him by our side.

In John 16:33, we are reminded of the words of Jesus when he said, "I have said these things to you, that in me you may have peace. In the world, you will find tribulation. But take heart! I have overcome the world."

When times get tough, good things actually start to happen and show up in our lives.

CONTROLLING OUR MINDSET

A great Stoic philosopher said,

"You have power over your mind - not outside events.
Realize this, and you will find strength."
—*Marcus Aurelius.*

This reminds us that our true power lies in controlling our reactions, not external circumstances. How we react gets placed in our minds, and if that reaction is worry, doubt, and trouble, we will feed more of it, and it will keep showing up on our doorstep.

In a world full of uncertainties, the ability to control our mindset is the ultimate strength as it helps us navigate life with resilience and peace. Worrying doesn't take away tomorrow's troubles, but it surely takes away today's peace. Worrying is like a rocking chair; it will give you something to do, but get you nowhere.

Seek to embrace the **PRESENT** because, in the end, that is all we have.

"Very little is needed to make a happy life;
it is all within yourself, in your way of thinking."

—Marcus Aurelius.

Happiness is not found in external circumstances but within ourself. By fostering a positive mindset, we can find joy and fulfillment in the present moment.

Our life becomes precisely and definitively what our thoughts make it, always has, always will. We can shape our reality by our vision and our thoughts. By aligning our thoughts with virtue, values, and purpose, we can create a life of meaning and fulfillment. Nowhere can you find a quieter or more peaceful place than in your own mind and soul. Live by virtue and values, and you will live a life of peace.

Our Mindset Matters.

WHATEVER THE MIND CAN CONCEIVE AND BELIEVE IT CAN ACHIEVE

Break down each word and define it.

Whatever...Mind...Can...Conceive...Believe...Achieve

- Whatever = *No limitation.*
- Mind = *That powerful place in between your ears.*
- Can = *A call to action. We always can.*
- Conceive = *To form or devise (a plan or idea) in the mind.*
- Believe = *Accept (something) as true; feel sure of the truth of something. Your opinion. YOUR acceptance.*
- Achieve = *successfully bring about or reach (a desired objective, level, or result) by effort, skill, or courage.*

There are no limitations to the mind, only to the body. If the mind can conceive it and then feed it with true belief and action, it can achieve the outcome. Live your life by this one simple concept, and you will reach great heights and fulfillment.

"First comes thought; then organization of that thought into ideas and plans; then transformation of those plans into reality. The beginning, as you will observe, is in your imagination." Napoleon Hill

It all starts with your vision and what you conceive. Believe it's possible, and you can create that future reality.

FEED THE RIGHT WOLF

Always remember,
you have control over which Wolf you feed,
and the choices you make will define who you are.

Two Wolves

One evening, an old Cherokee told his grandson about a battle that goes on inside people. He said, "My son, the battle is between two wolves inside us all.

One is EVIL. It is anger, jealousy, sorrow, regret, greed, arrogance, self-pity, guilt, resentment, inferiority, lies, false pride, superiority, and ego.

The other is GOOD. It is joy, peace, love, hope, serenity, humility, kindness, benevolence, empathy, generosity, truth, compassion, and faith."

The grandson thought about it for a minute and then asked his grandfather, "Which wolf wins?"

The old Cherokee simply replied, "The one you feed."

BELIEVE GOOD THINGS
WILL HAPPEN
AND THEY WILL

This is magical advice that can change everything. Start your day with the mindset that something wonderful will happen to you today.

Do this each morning and each day, saying it all throughout the day. Then, go throughout the day, always seeking that, and say to yourself, was this the something wonderful that I was thinking about? As you experience life, look for those magical things to happen. Before you go to sleep, believe that something wonderful is going to happen to you tomorrow.

All of a sudden, you will experience that your life is a series of wonderful, positive, happy experiences (the parking spot will open, the call from a friend will come, the teacher will be responsive, the grade you want will show up, etc.).

If you change the prism of your view (change what you see) and look for things that are wonderful, and then believe they will happen, the universe and God will place them right in your path. The universe wants to conspire for you to give you what you desire.

Believe Good Things Will Happen and They Will.

YOUR IMAGINATION IS YOURS

Everything that now exists was once imagined. Therefore, everything that is going to exist must first be imagined. If you can place what you want to attract into your imagination, it will chase after you. Then you feed it.

There is power in awareness and power in I AM (and whatever words follow). We understand from the words of Ephesians 5:13, "All things, when they are admitted, are made manifest by the light; for everything that is made manifest is light."

That which you FEEL yourself to be, you are, and you are given that which you are. Therefore, assume the feeling that would be yours as if you were already in possession of your wish, then your wish must be realized. Live in the feeling of being the one you want to be, and THAT'S WHO YOU SHALL BE.

I am healthy because I feel great. I feel healthy. I feel well. I live my life through a feeling in my body that I am strong and capable. Don't change your feelings based on what someone else says. Opinions of others don't count.

The only opinion that matters is yours.

GET COMFORTABLE
BEING UNCOMFORTABLE

Contrary to popular thinking, going easy is not the way. As stated earlier, no one remembers easy.

Going easy and avoiding difficult leads to mediocrity, complacency, and staleness. Instead, challenge yourself in different ways, with different ideas and different actions. Discomfort is not something we enjoy as humans, but it is a necessary ingredient in dealing with life's challenges.

We must experience discomfort. We must do things that are difficult. As you embrace these activities, think and feel you were practicing for this all along. In this exercise, you are training your body, mind, and spirit, as well as strengthening your attitude of perseverance and determination.

When you challenge your comfort zone and start to become comfortable being in that uncomfortable space, you train your mind to face these challenges with greater vigor, confidence, and tenacity. When we survive these uncomfortable moments and experiences, the relief becomes glorious, liberating, and worthwhile.

Start with yourself. Look inward and challenge the comfortable.

THE SECRET SAUCE OF LIFE

Is there a secret sauce that allows us to live the life we have imagined, or achieve all our hopes, dreams, and desires? I believe it exists in the LAG approach.

In understanding and studying the mind, the pitfalls of life, and the successes that abound, there are certain non-negotiable ingredients I believe may capture the secret sauce. When popularized, utilized, and magnetized each day, these three ingredients are sure to lead to a more positive outcome in achieving your hopes, dreams, and desires.

Love is the single most important ingredient of all. It all starts here. Love what you do. Love who you are. Love the people who support you and provide encouragement on your journey. When your heart is filled with love, your journey becomes fulfilled.

Attitude is an ingredient that we control. We can choose a positive attitude that lights up a room, smiles when spoken to, and emits energy to the world. It is our choice. You have all the power to make that choice.

Gratitude is the most important fundamental ingredient in everything. Being appreciative and grateful for everything is scientifically guaranteed to create a better mindset and better control of your emotions. A daily practice of gratitude keeps the mind in the right place. When the mind is in gratitude, it cannot be anywhere else, so the negative will not be present.

So, my secret sauce for life is LAG—Love, Attitude, and Gratitude. Try it, you might like it!

FREEDOM LIES IN THE SPACE
BETWEEN EVENT AND RESPONSE

There is a gap between the event and response to the event. That gap is your patience, faith, and freedom. To understand the language of faith, you need to have patience. This skill is the freedom to believe that the result is on the horizon at all times. We often become impatient as we seek results in our time frame instead of God's. If you patiently endure and consistently believe with unseen faith, you will experience it all, and your life will become more fulfilled.

Think of a baby crying for warm milk while you heat it. In your mind, you say, "Okay, give me a break; it's warming up." The baby does not understand that language and continues to wail, only to be soothed by the warm bottle when it is ready. That's how God's plan works for all of us. We wail and cry and sometimes stop short of the discipline and patience of our Faith. It is right before you stop short of faith that you must look inward and understand that with faith and patience, you will obtain all that you desire.

"Take the first step in faith. You don't have to see the whole staircase; just take the first step." Martin Luther King Jr.

Many times, we want to see the whole staircase, but the secret is that it will all work out according to God's plan. And if we can endure that through faith and patience, that experience is freedom.

BE THANKFUL
AND APPRECIATIVE

Appreciate and be gracious for what God gave you: the ability to achieve all you desire, play sports, and live life abundantly, enjoying all it has to offer. When you lose sight of this, reset your lens and go to a children's hospital. This will clearly refocus your mind and let you understand what is really important in life. In the end, most of those children who are sick would probably give a limb to experience the pleasures of our lives, which we sometimes take for granted.

In everything you do, give thanks. It is such an abundant and grateful way of living. Give thanks to God, and watch how all the universe smiles upon you and thanks you back. God and the universe are conspiring for you, so saying thank you is the polite thing to do in return.

THE SECRET TO SUCCESS

Defining success comes in all shapes and sizes, yet in my humble opinion, it has some simple principles at the core of its roots. To succeed in anything, the key is to be the best you can be without comparing yourself to anyone else. Be reminded that you control your effort to be the best. The way we get there is to maximize our potential through our best efforts. It is the maximum effort that counts most and offers the greatest fulfillment and the ultimate measure of success. Success is not defined by material things, money, power, or the aloof concepts most people think. Rather, it is more of an internal feeling and inner quality that shows up each day in the way you approach life.

While competition is the driving force, you must put all your effort into accomplishing success. The standard that eclipses the win is the effort to do the best you can. That is the true measure of success. If you have all the potential to be greater than you are, but consistently produce low-measured effort, you have not achieved success. On the other hand, if you have talent that is maximized each and every day, your view of the mirror looking back becomes quite pleasurable because you have achieved success.

Go out and compete against yourself every day in all that you do. Set your standards high and focus on the pursuit rather than the end. Continue the pursuit by challenging yourself to be slightly better than the day before. One day, you will wake up, look in the mirror, and feel fulfilled through the inner peace you have acquired.

When you do your best you will accomplish success.

JUST BELIEVE

T hings almost always work out the way they are supposed to, according to God's plan, usually based on the behavior of humans. We go through life expecting results but rarely look inward at the behavior and characteristics that guide that expectation. We meander through life, always responding to events and circumstances, getting angry, and believing things are happening to us as opposed to for us. One of the core principles of scripture reading is to Believe everything happens for you. Believe that there is a greater plan for you. Believe that as you walk the walk with integrity, goodness, faith, love and other good ingredients sprinkled in between, you will get exactly what you deserve.

God is committed to seeing you through the hard times and the troubles that show up each day. Seek a relationship with Him, stay close, and Believe. God and the universe are cheering you on and conspiring for you to be the best of which you are capable and to live life to the fullest. When you have love, patience, and faith, you will walk with inner peace knowing all that remains for you to do is believe. When that happens, you have arrived.

Everything is summed up with this final deliverable, Belief. With Belief, there is nothing you cannot accomplish. Belief is the locomotive that drives the freight train forward. When you surround Belief with the deliverables in this book, you will transform your life, find inner peace, and become the best version of yourself, "And will you succeed? Yes! You will, indeed! 98 and ¾ percent guaranteed." Dr. Seuss, *Oh, The Place You'll Go.*

AFTERWORD

My journey of learning came from books, great people, and life experiences. Indelibly etched in my mind and soul, and someone I will be grateful for until my days are gone, is Fr. Philip Eichner from Chaminade High School. He was my spiritual guide throughout high school, and I thank God for bringing him into my life because fate clearly crossed our paths. In that calm and confident voice, he said to me, "JOSEPH, life will hit you with challenges all the time, but remember the Lord and always look to do the right thing because it's the right thing to do, expecting nothing in return. You will mess up and you will make mistakes. As you go through life, try to make less and less of them. When you do that, all of a sudden, you will start to find some clarity in life and the things you do."

So, on my journey to find guidance, I developed a keen understanding of the mind, how it works, and how it translates into reality, and always wanted to share this information. I studied the mind, read countless books, became a certified mental training coach, and took a massive number of notes. Perhaps the best education I had was using these skills in everyday life, on the athletic field, in the courtroom, in life, and in business.

This book was written for the youth, for the young high school or college students. It's for athletes and non-athletes. Anyone will tell you that I think the greatest experience in life is being a student-athlete, not an athletic student, but a student-athlete.

I remain grateful and thankful.

A STORY ABOUT
THE FATHER OF FOUR GIRLS

As the father of four girls, life was filled with lots of talking, drama, opinions, and ideas. This required patience. They say that if you want patience, God does not make you patient but provides an opportunity to become patient. I am forever grateful to have experienced four daughters. It is the greatest achievement of my life. I embraced their love and witnessed their confusion. The journey of this path led me to see the world through a different prism; one with boundless energy, opportunity, and optimism.

My first daughter, Brianna, always loved the mind and the fascination of thoughts. Her big blue eyes, fiercely competitive spirit, and love of medicine always shined. We had an amazing bond as she studied neuroscience in college to become a surgeon. We enjoyed sports, competition, and watching the Yankees. I vividly remember her little feet hanging off the couch, watching the Yankees and cheering," Let's go 'Ankees.'"

I can confidently say that she had a lot of faith in my words in the field of competition. As her coach, I taught her to use her mindset to succeed in sports, because Mindset Matters.

One day, my daughter Kaitlin said, "I know you are all positive and stuff, but what do you do when you are positive and think you are going to win and then you don't?"

I responded, "I am never defeated, Kaitlin, unless I allow defeat to be accepted in my reality. Yes, I have failed, but defeat is a mere state of mind, and I trained myself not to get into that state of mind."

Kaitlin is a very faith-based person who takes her love of God seriously and has this great comedic personality. Her infectious smile can light up a room, and her inquisitive, investigative mind leads to a lot of questions. Another former student athlete, she has an inspiring vision for her future that is refreshing. At six years old, she would sit with a group of adult friends and have a conversation about the most mundane concepts. They loved it!

My daughter Julia often said, "Dad, what if I don't do well on this test? What if I don't pitch well? What if the other team wins?"

I always responded, "Julia, what if you do well on the test? What if you pitch well, and what if you win?"

We would have this debate often, but I would never give in. There were times when she would start the conversation and say, "Hey, Dad, don't tell me what if we win, but I am going to ask you a question. What if we don't win today?"

Obviously, I did not give in. I would smile at her and say, "Do you want my answer?"

You get the point. Eventually, Julia started, albeit at a snail's pace, to understand that Dad's mind just does not work that way. I wanted to train her mind not to work that way either and always look on the bright side. Because Mindset Matters.

My youngest daughter, Olivia, is a kind and gentle soul—not fiercely competitive but wildly loyal and loving. Our car ride talks are priceless as they delve into every day mundane aspects of life that often lead to God, Faith, practicing law, how to treat people, or just random stuff. We love enjoying funny riddles and coming up with creative inventions. We talk about mindset and the way people think, behave, react, and respond. Ironically, I have learned a lot from her.

My daughters have challenged me over and over. I can't say I have loved all the challenges, but I have definitely learned to appreciate them and be grateful because, through them, I had the opportunity to grow, learn, and develop.

I hear there is a special place in heaven for the father of four daughters. I hope so because it has been a wild ride with them.

Hakuna Matata!

ABOUT THE AUTHOR

Passion for anything he puts his mind to, and being a mindful follower of Jesus, is a great way to describe Coach Joe. Born in Brooklyn, NY, moving to the suburbs as a young boy, and attending an All-Boys catholic high school, his journey is long and winding. It has hills, valleys, and bends sideways. It has brought him to his knees, and at times, flowed a river of grief from his eyes. He has unending faith that things will work out the way they are supposed to according to God's Plan. Coach Joe says, "It's up to us to navigate the plan, make good choices, treat others with kindness and respect, and then see blessings in everything". In this, he believes we find inner peace.

This little book provides short stories of things he learned during his journey through life. Coach Joe reads scripture and journals, meditates, and looks in the mirror to find inner peace. As an attorney, entrepreneur, mindset coach, husband, father of four daughters, mentor, and friend, his days are filled. His goal is to forgive, love, be merciful to someone who needs it, and listen with two ears. This leads to inner peace. He has learned to change the prism of his view, and that has been the difference.

Joseph S. Maniscalco is a graduate of Fordham University (B.A.) (1992) and Hofstra Law School (J.D.) (1995). As a seasoned trial attorney, he continues to challenge his mind in high-pressure situations. As an entrepreneur, he has learned to listen to people and ask questions. His coaching days started in law school to earn extra money and continued as a young lawyer, making a minuscule salary. He has coached at the T-ball level and was blessed to have an opportunity to coach at the collegiate level. This little book has been germinating in his mind for many years, and the forces of nature and timing pushed him to bring it to the world. Sit back, read, think, analyze, and then seek the inner peace the short stories aim to provide.

www.ingramcontent.com/pod-product-compliance
Lightning Source LLC
Chambersburg PA
CBHW020920140626
46545CB00015B/1002